Yo, Millard Fillmore!

Will Cleveland & Mark Alvarez
Illustrations by Tate Nation

SCHOLASTIC INC.
New York Toronto London Auckland Sydney
Mexico City New Delhi Hong Kong Buenos Aires

W9-AXW-486

To Anne, Braden, Meg and Will

ISBN 0-439-58906-1

12 11 10 9 8 7 6 5 4 3 2 1   3 4 5 6 7 8/0

Printed in the U.S.A.   23

First Scholastic printing, September 2003

Cover illustration: Tate Nation
Cover design: Sharon Lane Holm
Book design: Deborah Fillion

Table of Contents

How to Use This Book
To Gain *Instant, Effortless* Knowledge

1. Read **only** the cartoons and their captions.

(**Don't** read the stuff on the left-hand pages.
That's for later.)

2. Take the little quizzes after every ten cartoons.

3. Try not to be *too* impressed with yourself
when you've memorized the Presidents **forever**
in twenty minutes.

That's it. Hot stuff, huh?

The Presidents. Right. Here's the way most Americans sound when they try to run through a list of these great (and not so great) Americans from start to finish. ("Let's see. Washington, hmm, hmm, Jefferson, hmm, hmm, Jackson, hmm, hmm, hmm, Lincoln, hmm, hmm, Teddy Roosevelt, hmm, hmm....")

For Adults Only

Naturally, this makes us feel rotten. We live our lives under a cloud of guilt brought on by forgetting whether Tyler comes before Taylor, or who was who among those bearded, late nineteenth century Republicans. We're terrified that we'll get on *Jeopardy* and stupidly confuse—in front of millions of viewers who will be blowing raspberries at the screen in living rooms all over America—Benjamin Harrison (number 23, 1889-1893) with his grandfather, William Henry Harrison (number 9, 1841).

INCREASE
your self esteem.

AMAZE
your friends.

Well, this book will shape all of us right up. Never again will we forget to tuck Franklin Pierce in there between our man Millard Fillmore and James Buchanan, or get Madison and Monroe settled in backward. We'll have all of this *down*. And, after years of angst, ignorance and guilt, we'll be able to relax.

It'll be even better for our kids. They'll get all this crammed into their craniums long before some colleague can turn to them over a lunchtime Perrier and embarrass them by asking, "Say, did Grant come before or after Hayes, anyway?"

Best of all, for adults or kids, is the fact that we can not only have a great loony time learning this stuff, but we can *show off* to all those people who haven't read this
book and who can't tell Polk from Harding.
Those dummies.

DAZZLE
your teachers.

GUARANTEE yourself
a life of SUCCESS and
HAPPINESS.

For Kids Only

So your dad or your grandmother bought you this book on the presidents. One more for the trash heap, right? Wrong. So wrong you can't believe it. This book is more about magic than it is about the presidents—brain magic.

What's more, this is a comic book.

And not *just* a comic book. Unless all the hours of TV have made you totally brain dead (TBD), you're going to be flat amazed at what this book can do. Once you've read this book once (maybe twice), you will know all of the presidents backwards and forwards. You will know them without trying and you will know them forever.

Life's tough. There's lots to do and not enough time to do it. You've always dreamed of being able to learn stuff without trying. Now's your chance. Don't blow it.

Except for the TBD, who take a little longer, you can read the cartoons in this book in about twenty minutes. In five minutes you will have, automatically and without trying, learned the first ten presidents. You don't believe it now, but it's true. How does it work? What can we say? It's a miracle.

Teachers and text book writers have spent centuries inventing the most incredibly boring way to talk about whatever it is they talk about. You wish it could be different. You think it could be different.

4

Would I lie?

It is.

Here.

Now.

Trust us. Unless you are TBD, your brain can do amazing things. We'll show you how.

One little word of caution! After the first three cartoons, you'll wonder whether we, the authors, aren't TBD. We're not. We're geniuses. But it is going to take going through the first ten cartoons for you to see why.

| BOREDOM ALERT! |

Read only the cartoons and their captions!

Don't bother with the other stuff until you feel like it.

5

George Washington

1732-1799   President 1789-1797

A lot of the old stories about our first President—like the one about the cherry tree—aren't true, but Washington is still "first in war, first in peace, and first in the hearts of his countrymen." Washington, who was so popular after the Revolution that he could have assumed the powers of a dictator, would never hear of such a thing. And although he could easily have been elected to a third term as President, he declined to run. He felt that our new country's success and greatness depended on its ideals, its laws and its representative form of government, not on his personal leadership—or on anybody's. By his example, Washington estab-

lished the tradition of a peaceful transfer of power from one President to the next. A man of great honor, dignity, courage and principle, Washington remains the greatest of all American heroes.

Washington's very first military command ended in total disaster. During the French and Indian War, he chose the worst possible site to build a fortification called Fort Necessity near present-day Pittsburgh, and he was soon forced to surrender it to the French. Later, during the Revolution, he was often discouraged, but never as deeply as at Fort Necessity.

1. George Washington

(Okay, okay. You don't need this book to remind you who the first President was. But it's a good idea to start from the beginning, so hang in here with us.)

The Presidents live in the White House, in Washington, D.C. Imagine on the lawn of the White House a huge washing machine big enough to **wash a ton** of clothes.

Wash a ton
for Washington.

John Adams

1735-1826

President 1797-1801

John Adams was smarter than Washington, and just as honest, but he was also cranky, vain and no great leader of men. He was one of the earliest to come out in favor of American independence, he nominated Washington to command American forces in the Revolution, and he helped negotiate the peace treaty that made the United States a sovereign nation. He served as Washington's Vice President for eight years, but despite his integrity and his record, he didn't have the talent to make people like him, and he was never a popular President in his own right.

Adams was from Massachusetts—the only non-Virginian among our first five Presidents. He was the first to live in the White House. The building wasn't finished when he and his wife, Abigail, moved in, and she could find nowhere suitable to dry their laundry, so she hung it up in the East Room, which is now the site of state dinners and receptions. Adams died at 90, until Ronald Reagan the longest-lived of all our Presidents.

2. John Adams

Imagine that when you raise the lid of the washing machine and look inside, there are a lot of **atoms** swirling around in the water.

Atoms
for Adams.

Thomas Jefferson

1743-1826   President 1801-1809

Jefferson was always prouder to have written the Declaration of Independence and founded the University of Virginia than he was to have been President. During his administration, the U.S. purchased the Louisiana Territory, which almost doubled the size of the United States. Jefferson sent Lewis and Clark west to explore the vast new territory, and today you can see many of the artifacts they brought back at Monticello, Jefferson's home near Charlottesville, VA.

Jefferson was interested in—and talented at—almost everything under the sun, from agriculture and architecture to zoology. In the early 1960s, President Kennedy once entertained a number of distinguished intellectuals at a White House dinner. In his toast he said that the White House had not seen such brain power gathered together "since Thomas Jefferson dined here alone."

What's this?
Well, now the atoms are
being fried up over a grill by
a **chef's son** who is wearing
his father's big chef's hat.

Chef's son
for Jefferson.

James Madison

1751-1836

President 1809-1817

Because of his efforts in drafting, negotiating and defending it, Madison is known as "The Father of the Constitution." He was President during the War of 1812 (which was called "Mr. Madison's War" by its many opponents), when the British captured Washington and burned the Capitol and the White House. First Lady Dolley Madison escaped just before the British arrived, and she took with her the famous Stuart portrait of George Washington, saving it from destruction.

Madison was the shortest of our Presidents, at 5 foot 4, and he weighed only a little over 100 pounds. Dolley Madison was the first person to serve ice cream in the White House. She was always a popular figure in Washington, and many years after her husband died, she was voted an honorary seat on the floor of the House of Representatives.

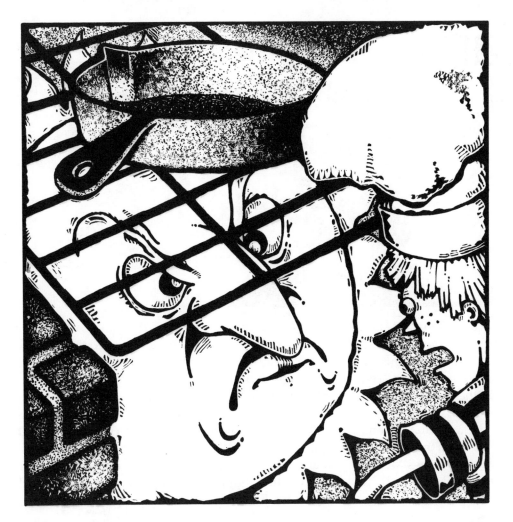

4. James Madison

Look under the grill.
That's one **mad sun** trapped
in there and forced to make
heat for the cook!

Mad sun
for Madison.

James Monroe

1758-1831

President 1817-1825

Monroe was President during what's remembered as "the Era of Good Feelings," after the country's early disputes had largely been settled and before the disagreements between North and South had become serious. In fact, feelings were so good that when he ran for his second term, he was unopposed. While Monroe was President, the United States declared that it would not allow any European countries to further colonize North or South America. This was the famous Monroe Doctrine. (But you knew that already, didn't you?)

Monroe was wounded in the Battle of Trenton, which was the battle Washington crossed the Delaware to fight, and the musket ball remained in his shoulder for the rest of his life. But Washington wasn't always as proud of Monroe as he was after that battle. When Monroe was the U.S. Ambassador to France in the mid-1790s, he publicly criticized the Jay Treaty between the United States and Britain. President Washington was so angry at him that he removed him from office and ordered him home. We forget sometimes that the "Founding Fathers" didn't always agree or get along!

5. James Monroe

Well, the mad sun has escaped—but he's still hot! He opens his mouth and out flows a boiling river. In the river is some **money row**-ing a boat.

Money row
for Monroe.

Take a look at that money: it's a **five** dollar bill. This is a quick way to remember that Monroe was the **fifth** President.

15

John Quincy Adams

1767-1848

President 1825-1829

John Quincy Adams was, until George W. Bush took office in 2001, part of the only father-son act in Presidential history. Like his father, he was a man of great dignity and integrity. But, also like his father, he was a lousy politician. Here's what he said about himself: "I am a man of reserved, cold, austere and forbidding manners." No wonder John Quincy joined his father as the only one-term Presidents among the first six men to hold the office. After being defeated for reelection as President, John Quincy Adams was elected to the House of Representatives and served there until he died, a fierce and aggressive opponent of slavery.

As a boy living near Boston, Adams watched the entrenched Americans mow down line after line of advancing British soldiers at the Battle of Bunker Hill in 1775. As President, he installed the first billiard table in the White House. In Washington, Adams liked to skinny dip in the Potomac River early in the morning. One day a newspaperwoman named Anne Royall followed him there and sat on his clothes until he agreed to give her an interview. He finally answered her questions standing stark naked and chin-deep in the water. A bit different from the modern Presidential news conferences we see on TV!

6. John Quincy Adams

Uh-oh!
The money rowing can't see where it's going, and it bumps into **a dam**.

A dam
for Adams.

Andrew Jackson

1767-1845

President 1829-1837

Jackson was the last Revolutionary War veteran to serve as President. He was known as "Old Hickory" because of his toughness as a soldier, and he was a tough, combative President, too. He once threatened to hang South Carolina leaders who were seeking to "nullify" a federal law. Jackson saw himself as the first "people's President"—the first Chief Executive to rise out of the rough-and-tumble of the western frontier rather than the easier living of the long-settled coast.

Jackson was famous for getting into fights. In 1806, he fought a duel with a man named Charles Dickenson, who had insulted his beloved wife, Rachel. Dickenson, known as the best shot in the country, fired first and hit Jackson in the chest. Jackson managed to stand, then fired and killed Dickenson. The pistol ball remained in Jackson's lung for the rest of his life. Jackson was shot in the arm in another gunfight in 1813. The ball wasn't removed until 1832. A very tough cookie, old Andy.

Now, instead of water flowing over a dam, imagine the jack of spades, the jack of diamonds and the other **jacks** from a deck of playing cards tumbling over.

Jacks
for Jackson.

Martin van Buren

1782-1862   President 1837-1841

Van Buren had been Jackson's Vice President. He was the last Vice President before George Bush who was elected to succeed the President before him. He shares another similarity with George Bush: he was blamed for the hard economic times that began soon after he was elected, and was defeated in his bid for reelection. He tried, but failed to get his party's nomination in 1844, so in 1848 he ran—and lost—on the Free Soil ticket.

Van Buren, who spoke Dutch at home, was the first President born in the United States of America. The others hadn't been born in another *place*, just in another *time*—before the colonies declared their independence. He was known as "Old Kinderhook" for his hometown in New York, and it is said that the expression okay came from his habit of scratching "O.K." in the margins of state documents to indicate his approval. (This is one of those stories that probably isn't true, but that's too good to ignore.)

8. Martin van Buren

The jacks are having an identity crisis—they think they're car jacks and they turn up next in place of tires on a van! (They must give a pretty bumpy ride, don't you think?) Riding around on top of the van is a big old bureau. Why is it up there? Easy—it's a **van bureau**!

Van bureau
for van Buren.

William Henry Harrison

1773-1841   President 1841

Harrison was the only President whose father signed the Declaration of Independence. Until Ronald Reagan, he was the oldest President at his inauguration—68. There's not much else to say about Harrison as President, because he wasn't around long. He made a very long inaugural address on a very cold day, developed pneumonia, and died only a month after he took office. He was the first President to die in office, and he served the shortest term of any President.

Harrison won office on the most famous campaign slogan in American history: "Tippecanoe and Tyler, too," Harrison was known as "Old Tippecanoe" because, as a general, he had defeated the Indian chief Tecumseh at a battle on the Tippecanoe River in Indiana Territory.

9. William Henry Harrison

Oh no!
Wild hair is sprouting all over everything. What we've got here is a **hairy van**.

Hairy van
for Harrison.

John Tyler

1790-1862 President 1841-1845

Being "Tyler, too" isn't quite as zippy as being Old Tippecanoe. But a President had never before died in office, and no one expected Tyler to become President—least of all the Whigs who nominated him, but with whom he had serious disagreements. When he vetoed a bill to resurrect the Bank of the United States—a basic Whig policy—all but one member of his cabinet resigned. He came to be known as "the President without a party."

Tyler was the first President to be married in the White House. He was also the President with the most children—15 in all (eight from his first marriage and seven from his second—eight were boys and seven were girls). Tyler was the only former President to side with the South during the Civil War. He was elected to the Confederate Congress in 1862, although he died before he could take his seat.

10. John Tyler

Somebody's taken all that hair and woven it together into a man's necktie! And that tie has a fishing lure stuck to it! Of course, it's not just any old fishing lure, it's a **tie lure**.

Tie lure
for Tyler.

How old are boys when they have to start wearing ties? **Ten** years old, right? Well, that's as good an age as any, and a lucky thing too.
Now you can remember that President Tie-lure was the **tenth** President.

Quiz #1

Let's take a break and see what you have learned.

Thinking about the first President, what is in front of the White House?

What is inside the washing machine?

Who's cooking the atoms?

What provides the heat for the grill?

What is in the boiling river coming out of the mad sun's mouth?

What denomination is the money rowing the boat?

(That tells you that Monroe was what number President?)

What does the money row boat bump into?

What is flowing over the dam?

Where do the four jacks turn up?

What happens to the van and the bureau?

What does the hair turn into?

How old did we decide a boy is when he starts wearing a tie?

(Tyler is what number President?)

NICE WORK!

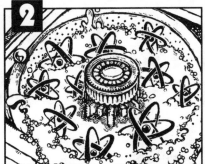

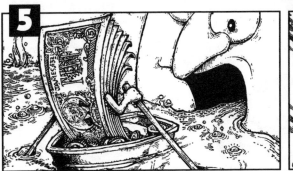

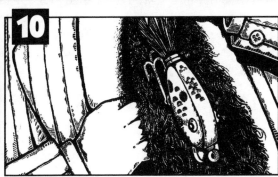

James K. Polk

1795-1849   President 1845-1849

You'll sometimes hear Polk called our greatest one-term President. He avoided war with Britain in 1846, by agreeing to split the Oregon Territory (now Oregon, Washington and part of British Columbia) along the 49th parallel, rather than holding out for a boundary along the latitude 54° 40'. In doing so, he put to rest the popular war cry, "Fifty-four forty or fight!" Polk was President during the Mexican War, which opponents called "Mr. Polk's War." Abraham Lincoln, who was a Congressman at the time, bitterly opposed the war, which he considered immoral and unconstitutional. U.S. Grant also felt that the war was wrong, although as a soldier he fought in it. Polk chose not to run for a second term, and died the same year he left office.

Polk is the only man to have served as both President and Speaker of the House of Representatives. His wife, Sarah, held the first annual Thanksgiving dinner at the White House, and, like John Tyler, she supported the Confederacy during the Civil War.

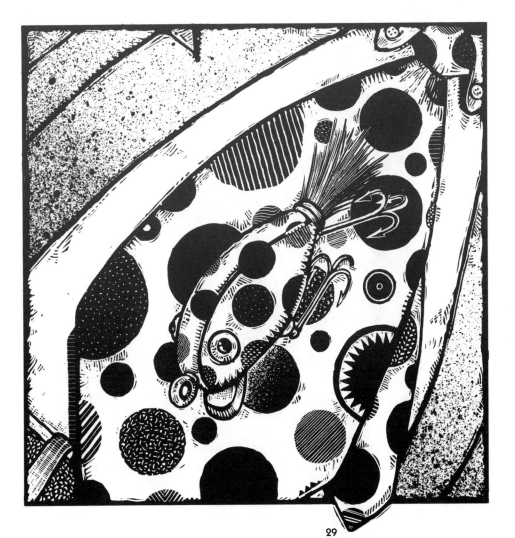

Take another look at the tie and the lure, but this time focus on the big **polka dots** all over them.

Polka dots
for Polk.

Zachary Taylor

1784-1850

President 1849-1850

Taylor became a national hero as a general during the Mexican War. He was known as "Old Rough and Ready." Because he was always on the move as a professional soldier, the first Presidential election he voted in was his own. This was the first year that voting took place on a single day, rather than over a period of several. Although he held many slaves himself, Taylor opposed the spread of slavery, which was *the* hot issue of his era.

Taylor was the first President never to serve in either the Continental Congress, the Senate or the House of Representatives. Jefferson Davis, the future President of the Confederacy, eloped with Taylor's daughter, Sarah, in 1835. In 1991, Zachary Taylor's body was removed from its tomb and tested for poison. A historian had a theory that Taylor had been quietly murdered by political enemies who favored the expansion of slavery into the territories and new states. The tests showed no evidence of poison.

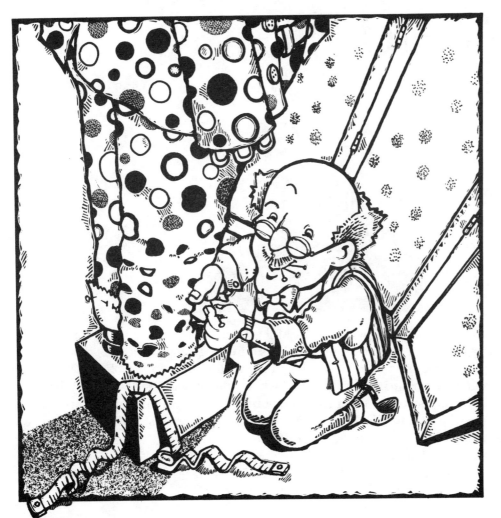

That polka dot material is so neat that a **tailor** has decided to make a suit out of it.

Tailor
for Taylor.

Millard Fillmore

1800-1874   President 1850-1853

Yo, Millard! Fillmore was the first President born in the 1800s and the last Whig President. Commodore Perry made his famous visit to Japan during Fillmore's administration. His party wouldn't renominate him for a new term in 1852 because of his support for the Compromise of 1850, which included the Fugitive Slave Act. The law said that a slave who escaped to a free state must still be returned to his owner. Fillmore tried to become President again in 1856 as the candidate of the Know-Nothing Party. He lost.

Millard was Fillmore's mother's maiden name. He was born in a log cabin which, for a while, seemed to be a near requirement for any President. The myth is that while Fillmore was President, the White House got its first bathtub with running water, but this was a joke concocted by the journalist and essayist H. L. Mencken in 1917.

13. Millard Fillmore

Golly, this tailor runs a service station, too. Watch him **fill more** and more little cups with a gasoline nozzle.

Fill more
for Fillmore.

Franklin Pierce

1804-1869   President 1853-1857

Pierce, sometimes known as "Handsome Frank," was 48 when he took office—the youngest President up to that time. As President, he failed to come to grips with the terrible problems that would soon result in Civil War, and his own party refused to renominate him in 1856. He remains the only elected President who was not renominated by his party when he wanted to run again for a second consecutive term.

Pierce's Vice President, William R. King, took his oath of office in Havana, Cuba, where he'd gone in the hopes of a tuberculosis cure. He is the only President or Vice President to be sworn in in a foreign country. Pierce's son, Bennie, was killed in a train crash just before Pierce took office. Neither Pierce nor his wife, who were riding near Bennie, was seriously injured. He was the third of their three children to die.

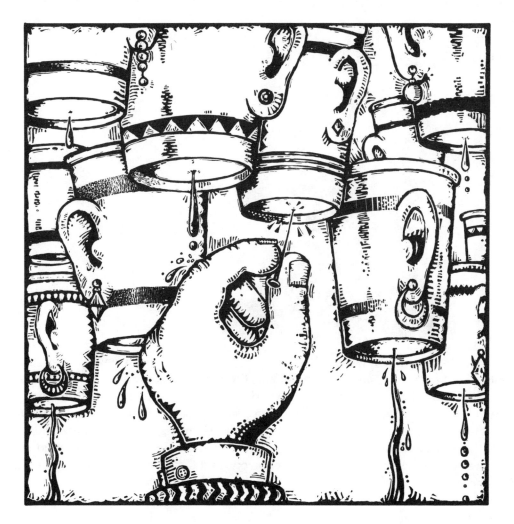

Notice that the little cups have ears for handles, and that the ears have all been **pierced** for earrings. The bottoms of the paper cups are being **pierced**, too, with a pin.

Pierced
for Pierce.

James Buchanan

1791-1868   President 1857-1861

Buchanan was the last of three successive undistinguished pre-Civil War Presidents. Like Pierce and others before him, he failed to resolve the quarrel between
North and South that was tearing the country apart. In
retrospect, many historians have felt that none of the
men *could* have succeeded—that the division between
the sections was so deep that the war was inevitable.

Buchanan was nearsighted in one eye and farsighted
in the other. He was the only President who never married. As a young man, he'd been engaged to Anne
Coleman, and there are many stories about why they
never married. In some, Buchanan broke the engage-
ment. In some, Anne did. In others, it was Anne's father's fault. But all the stories agree that a few months
afterwards, Anne died. Some say she committed sui-
cide in her sorrow, and that Buchanan mourned her for
the rest of his life.

15. James Buchanan

Careful!
The liquid from the pierced cups is dripping slowly into the barrels of U-shaped weapons below. What are those things, anyway? Right! They're **U-cannons**.

U-cannons
for Buchanan.

How much do you suppose a U-cannon's cannon ball weighs? Right! **Fifteen** pounds (if you're not convinced, just look at them). That's really handy, because Buchanan was the **fifteenth** President.

Abraham Lincoln

1809-1865   President 1861-1865

You know all about Honest Abe already, we hope! But did you know that his Gettysburg Address took only about a minute to deliver? Photographers couldn't even set up their cameras in time to get a picture of him speaking! Mostly because it was so short, many newspapers called his powerful words "embarrassing" and "silly." Just goes to show that you shouldn't believe everything you read.

Lincoln began as a Whig, but became a Republican shortly after the party was formed, and was the first Republican President. At 6 foot 4, Lincoln is the tallest man ever to have served as President. That's still awfully tall, but in 1861, it was *gigantic*. In fact, because of his height, his homeliness and his rumpled awkwardness, he was called a "baboon," a "gorilla" and an "orangutan" by his political opponents. See? Even great Presidents (maybe *especially* great Presidents) have their enemies.

16. Abraham Lincoln

Imagine all those cannons surrounding a **Lincoln Log® cabin** about to blow it up.

Lincoln Log cabin for Lincoln.

Andrew Johnson

1808-1875

President 1865-1869

Andrew Johnson became President when Lincoln was assassinated. He was a Southerner, a Democrat and a Unionist, a combination of traits that Lincoln thought could be important in helping to re-unite the divided country. He disagreed with many Congressional policies, and he was eventually impeached (tried before the Senate) for not bowing to its will. He escaped removal from office by a single vote. He wasn't nominated by the Democrats to run in 1868, but in 1874 he became the only former President to be elected to the Senate.

Johnson was taught to read and write by his future wife when he was 17 years old. He was the first true Presidential baseball fan—in 1867, he was guest of honor at a game between the Mutuals of New York and the Washington Nationals. It was during Johnson's administration that the U.S. bought Alaska. The purchase, negotiated by Secretary of State William H. Seward, was called by opponents "Seward's Folly."

Look!
On top of the Lincoln Log cabin is a big toilet, or john, and a little john. What's that little john doing up there? Well, it's the big **john's son**.

John's son
for Johnson.

Ulysses S. Grant

1822-1885

President 1869-1877

Grant was a natural to run for President in 1868, because he was the Union's greatest hero of the Civil War. He was always personally very popular, just as he was personally honest, but many of his appointees and associates were greedy crooks. As a result, his administration is remembered for its spectacular corruption.

Grant was only 5 foot 1 when he entered West Point!

(While he was there, he grew to 5 foot 7. Whew!) He wasn't a very good student, but he was a magnificent horseman. When the Civil War started, Grant had left the army and was working in his brothers' leather-goods store for $50 a month. Grant was tone deaf. He always said that he knew two songs: "One is Yankee Doodle," he'd say, "and the other isn't."

42

18. Ulysses S. Grant

Yuk!
Straining and wiggling to get out of the johns are enormous bugs that are known to science as "colonial hymenopterous insects," but we just call them **Great Ants**. (Say "Great Ants" ten times as fast as you can and see what you get.)

Great Ants
for Grant.

Rutherford B. Hayes

1822-1893   President 1877-1881

Hayes won the election of 1876 even though he had fewer popular votes (4,036,572) than his opponent, Samuel J. Tilden of New York (4,284,020). But Tilden was one short of a majority of Electoral ballots, and because of some serious hank-panky in Congress, Hayes emerged the victor after months of haggling. Hayes was never popular with many of the most powerful members of his own party, who weren't as interested as he was in reforming the corruption of the Grant administration. He announced at the beginning of his first term that he wouldn't seek a second.

Hayes was a general in the Civil War, and was badly wounded. He had horses shot from beneath him four times. His wife, Lucy, was the first First Lady to have graduated from college. A teetotaler and prohibitionist, Lucy Hayes forbade alcoholic drinks in the White House. As a result, she was known as "Lemonade Lucy." During the Hayes administration, the first telephone was installed in the White House, and inventor Thomas Edison personally demonstrated his new phonograph.

19. Rutherford B. Hayes

Watch out!
The Great Ants are free!
Luckily, they leave you alone
and crawl up the side of a
big **haystack**.

Haystack
for Hayes.

James Garfield

1831-1881 President 1881

Garfield was the third President in a row to have been a general during the Civil War. Part of a President's job in those days was to personally appoint people to government positions. Garfield was assassinated in Washington's Union Station by a man he'd refused to hire.

Andrew Jackson was the first President to have been born in a log cabin. Garfield was the last. He was also the first sitting member of the House of Representatives to be elected President. Our first left-handed Chief Executive, Garfield could write simultaneously in Latin with one hand and Greek with the other.

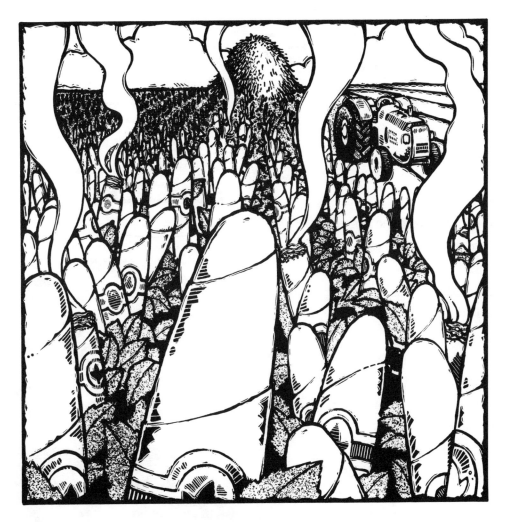

20. James Garfield

Hey!
What kind of place is this?
The haystack is at the end of
an odd field with cigars
growing out of the ground.
Why, it's a **cigar field**!

Cigar field
for Garfield.

The very best cigar boxes
have **twenty** cigars (enough
to make most people real
sick), which lets you know
that Garfield was the
twentieth President.

Quiz #2

Let's go over all the Presidents since Tyler.

What does the tie have all over it?
Who is fixing the polka dot suit?
What does the tailor do with the gasoline nozzle?
What happens to the filled cups?
Where does the liquid from the pierced cups drip?
How much do the cannon balls for the U-shaped cannons weigh?
(What number President is Buchanan?)

Where are the cannons aimed?
What is on top of the Lincoln Log cabin?
What is crawling out of the johns?
What do the Great Ants crawl up?
What is in the field with the haystack?
How many cigars are there in a really fine cigar box?
(What number President is Garfield?)

HOME RUN!

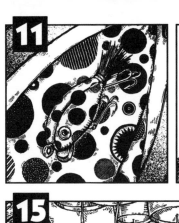
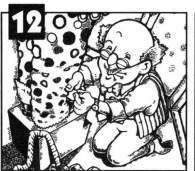

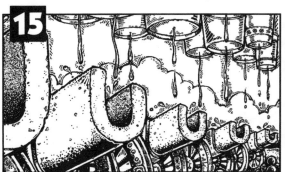

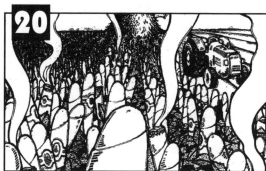

Chester A. Arthur

1830-1886

President 1881-1885

Known as "Chet" or "the General," Arthur was a machine politician from New York whom virtually everyone thought would be a disaster when Garfield's assassination elevated him to the Presidency. But he surprised everybody, turned against his crooked old friends and ran an honest, if undistinguished, administration. That's one reason why he wasn't nominated at the Republican convention in 1884.

There's some uncertainty about Arthur's year of birth. Some references say 1829. Some say 1830. But we don't fool around—we went right to the Manuscript Division of the Library of Congress. They say 1830. As a student at Union College, Arthur once stole the school bell and sank it in the Erie Canal. As an adult, he was a handsome and well-dressed man who liked good food, good music and good times. He enjoyed throwing parties at the White House a lot more than he enjoyed working there. In fact, one observer said of him that "President Arthur never did today what he could put off until tomorrow."

21. Chester A. Arthur

Whoops!
One of the cigars from the
cigar field has wandered off.
There he is—sitting at a
typewriter writing
a book. He is an **author**.

Author
for Arthur.

Grover Cleveland

1837-1908

President 1885-1889
1893-1897

As mayor of Buffalo and Governor of New York, Cleveland was known as "Grover the Good" because he had developed a ferocious reputation for honesty and efficiency. "A public office," he said, "is a public trust." This, along with a split in the Republican party, helped him become the first elected Democratic President since before the Civil War. When he ran for a second term in 1888, he won the popular vote, but lost (honestly, unlike Tilden) in the Electoral College.

Cleveland entered his first term as a bachelor, but he soon married 21-year-old Frances Folsom, whom he'd known since she was a baby. This was the first time a President was married in the Executive Mansion. Both of Cleveland's brothers were killed in 1872 when a ship they were on caught fire. When he was Sheriff of Erie County long before he became President, Cleveland acted as executioner at several hangings.

22. Grover Cleveland

Now imagine yourself looking down from an airplane. From your vantage point, you see the huge typewriter that Arthur the author was using sitting on a hillside. The landscape all around is filled with large single leaves standing on end. The typewriter is in **Leaf Land**!

Leaf Land
for Cleveland.

Benjamin Harrison

1833-1901   President 1889-1893

Harrison was the last Civil War general to be President. He wasn't a popular man—he was known as "the human iceberg" for his cold personality—but he was respected for his integrity. Six states (North Dakota, South Dakota, Montana, Washington, Idaho and Wyoming) were admitted to the union during Harrison's term—more stars added to the flag than during any other administration.

Harrison was the last of all those late nineteenth century Presidents to wear a beard—a tradition that dated back to Lincoln. Mrs. Harrison put up the first Christmas tree in the White House. Benjamin was the grandson of William Henry Harrison—the only grandfather-grandson combination we've had. Can you name the two sets of fathers and sons who have held the office?

23. Benjamin Harrison

Leaf Land has a problem. Just over the hill lives a giant hare and all of her sons. The **hare's sons** like nothing better than to hop from leaf to leaf nibbling on the very tastiest parts.

Hare's sons
for Harrison.

Grover Cleveland

1837-1908

He's back! Cleveland is the only President ever to win two terms that weren't in a row. His second term was marked by a serious depression, which cost him a lot of his popularity. Probably because he was known as a "sound money man," who opposed going off the Gold Standard, Grover Cleveland's picture is on the $1,000 bill.

In 1893, it was discovered that Cleveland had cancer of the jaw, and he was operated on in secret on a boat in New York's East River. The operation, which replaced part of the President's jaw with rubber, was a success, but it wasn't made known to the public until 1917. Cleveland's daughter, Esther, was the first child of a President to be born in the White House. His daughter Ruth, who was born in 1891 while he was out of office, had a candy bar named after her. Can you guess which one? Right! *Baby Ruth!*

56

24. Grover Cleveland

Watch out, hare's sons! Here comes a huge lamb who enjoys chopping up rabbits for dinner with his cleavers. Who is this meanie? You guessed it: **Cleaver lamb.**

Cleaver lamb
for Cleveland.

William McKinley

1843-1901

President 1897-1901

McKinley, who was the last President to have fought in the Civil War, was President during the Spanish American War, during which the U.S. gained control of the Philippines, Puerto Rico and Guam—its first overseas possessions. As he was shaking hands at the Pan-American Exposition in Buffalo, New York, McKinley was assassinated by a man who had concealed a pistol under a bandage he'd wrapped around his hand.

McKinley could write his name simultaneously with both hands. He'd write normally, from left to right, with his right hand, and backwards, from right to left, with his left hand (what *is* it with these Presidents and their oddball writing?). Another strong Gold Standard man, his picture's on the $500 bill.

Cleaver lamb has gone to town. There he is, in front of a McDonald's™, chopping up kindling wood. What would you call kindling from McDonald's? Why, **McKindling**, of course!

McKindling
for McKinley.

Under the McDonald's sign it shows that **25** billion McKindlings have been sold. That's because McKinley was the **twenty-fifth** President.

Theodore Roosevelt

1858-1919   President 1901-1909

There's simply too much to say about Teddy Roosevelt, who probably lived the most active, varied and interesting life of any Chief Executive. TR was an aggressive President who knew exactly what he wanted to get done. He used the "bully pulpit" of the Presidency to push through the Panama Canal. (Try this: spell "A man, a plan, a canal: Panama!" backwards—ignore the punctuation marks—and see what you get. Neat, huh? It's called a "palindrome," and it refers to TR.) He was also our greatest conservationist President, who believed in the need to set great parcels of land aside as parks and wilderness.

The teddy bear was named after Roosevelt. TR used to wrestle and play with his children in the White House. "You must always remember," said a British diplomat, "that the President is about six." TR's daughter, Alice, was a handful. When a friend chided him for not controlling her, Roosevelt said, "I can do one of two things. I can be President of the United States or I can control Alice. I cannot possibly do both."

Whoa!
A six foot teddy bear is in McDonald's ordering his food—and some of that gooooood McKindling. He is wearing a belt made out of bright red roses—**Teddy's rose belt**!

Teddy's rose belt
for Roosevelt.

William Howard Taft

1857-1930 President 1909-1913

Taft was elected with Roosevelt's help, but he disappointed his old friend, who felt he was getting too cozy with big business. As a result, Roosevelt ran against him in 1912 on the "Bull Moose" ticket. Both Wilson and Roosevelt out-polled Taft, the incumbent. Taft was the first President of all 48 contiguous states.

Taft was a gigantic man. He weighed over 300 pounds. He was the first of many Presidents to play golf regularly, and he originated the Presidential custom of throwing out the first ball of the baseball season—easier to do in the days when Washington had a team! In 1921, Taft was appointed Chief Justice of the Supreme Court by President Harding. He's the only man to hold both positions. As Chief Justice, he swore in both Calvin Coolidge (for his second term) and Herbert Hoover.

27. William Howard Taft

Imagine that Teddy rose belt is riding down a fast churning river in a rubber **raft** named Taffy.

Raft
for Taft.

Woodrow Wilson

1856-1924

President 1913-1921

Wilson was the first Southerner to be elected President since before the Civil War (he'd been born and raised in Virginia, even though he came to live in New Jersey). Although he campaigned in 1916 on the slogan, "He kept us out of war," he was forced to lead the country into World War I in 1917. He's best remembered for his "Fourteen Points," which he hoped would lead to a just and long-lasting peace. Wilson was awarded the Nobel Peace Prize in 1920.

Wilson was the last President to remember the Civil War personally. He was the first President to cross the Atlantic while he was in office—on his way to the Paris Peace Conference in 1919. He was also the first President to speak on the radio (can you guess who was the first to appear on TV? Don't worry—we'll tell you when the time comes.), and the first to hold a formal press conference. During his administration, the Nineteenth Amendment was passed, finally giving women the vote.

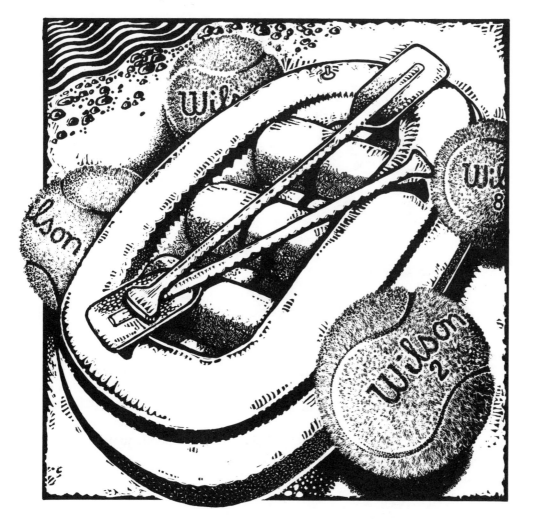

28. Woodrow Wilson

Now the raft begins to change. It sprouts wheels made out of tennis balls. What kind of tennis balls? Why, **Wilson**™, of course!

Wilson tennis balls for Wilson.

Warren G. Harding

1865-1923   President 1921-1923

Harding was a handsome, likable man, who was the first sitting Senator to be elected President. He promised the country a "return to normalcy" after the upheaval of World War I, and instead gave it one of the most corrupt administrations it its history, culminating in the famous Teapot Dome scandal. Harding died on his way home from a trip to Alaska before the scandal could touch him personally, but he's still generally considered the worst President in American history.

Harding was the first President to have a radio in the White House. He was also the first to visit Alaska and Canada while in office. Harding called his wife, "the Duchess." The G. stood for "Gamaliel"—Harding had been given his middle name in honor of his uncle, who was a chaplain at a state penitentiary.

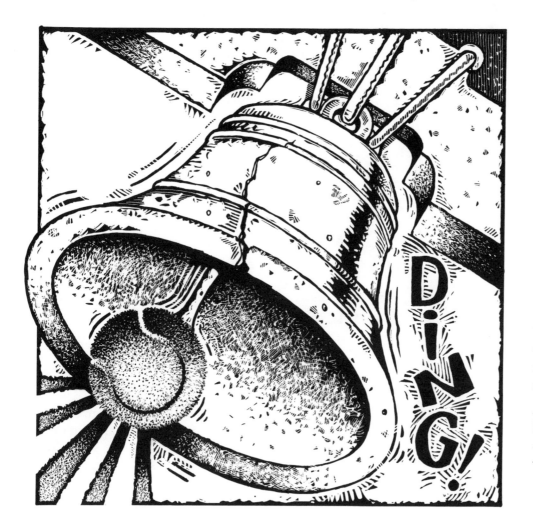

One of the tennis balls has somehow gotten attached to the end of a stone bell's clapper. The bell—being stone—rings with a **hard ding**.

Hard ding
for Harding.

Calvin Coolidge

1872-1933

President 1923-1929

Coolidge was a laconic Yankee who was known as "Silent Cal." He became a national figure when he broke a police strike in Boston, declaring, "There is no right to strike against the public safety by anybody, anywhere, anytime." Coolidge was home in Vermont when word came of Harding's death, and he was sworn in by his father, a justice of the peace. He took the oath in the middle of the night by the light of a kerosene lamp on his family's Bible. He didn't do much as President. That was the point.

Coolidge is the only President to have been born on the Fourth of July. He liked to get nine hours of sleep every night, and he usually took a two-hour nap in the afternoon. Once, old Silent Cal was seated next to a woman at a dinner party. She looked at him and said, "You know, my friends have bet me that I can't make you say three words all night, but I say I can." Coolidge looked back at her and said, "You lose."

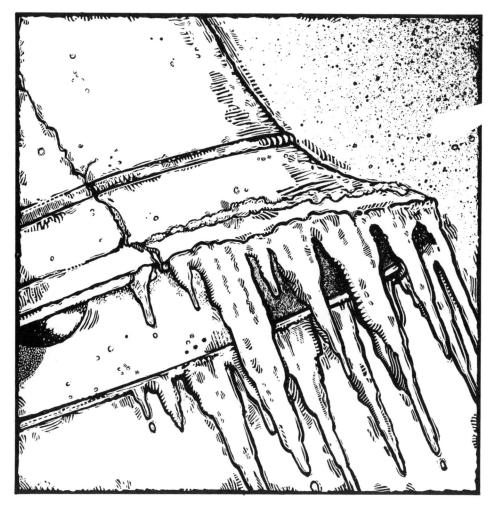

30. Calvin Coolidge

Brrr!
It's cold outside. In fact, the bell has icicles dripping from it—it has a **cool edge**.

Cool edge
for Coolidge.

For those icicles to form, how cool does the cool edge need to be? A little cooler than thirty-two degrees, right? Let's say a nice round **thirty** degrees. What a coincidence! Calvin Coolidge happens to have been our **thirtieth** President!

Quiz #3

Let's do a little review of the Presidents since Garfield.

What does the cigar become?

Where does his typewriter go?

What likes to eat the leaves?

Who scares off the hare's sons?

What does the Cleaver lamb chop up at work?

How many McKindlings have been sold?

(What number President is McKinley?)

What is inside McDonald's and what is he wearing?

What does the rose belt ride in?

What is on the corners of the raft?

Where does one of the tennis balls go and what sound does it make?

What happens to the edge of the bell?

How cold must it have been for the icicles to form?

(What number President is Coolidge?)

BULLY!

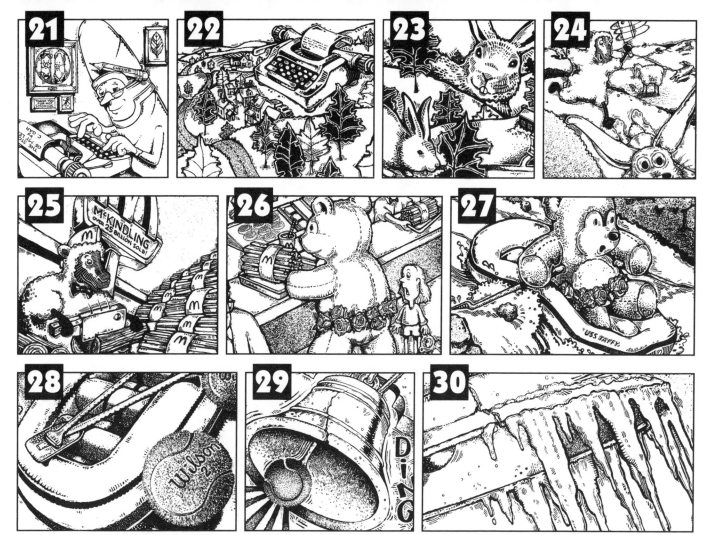

Herbert Hoover

1874-1964

President 1929-1933

Hoover was an Iowan—the first President born west of the Mississippi. Soon after he became President, the stock market crash plunged the nation into the Great Depression, which was to last throughout the 1930s. Martin Van Buren could have told Hoover how people would react. Right! He was thrashed in the election of 1932. Both before and after he was President, he was associated with great humanitarian relief work abroad, mainly to help the victims of World Wars I and II.

Hoover was perhaps the most successful self-made man ever to become President. He made several million dollars as a mining engineer before the First World War. Hoover lived for 31 years after he left office—the longest of any President. He died when he was 90, the second of three presidents to reach that age. Can you name the one who came before Hoover? (Hint: his son was President, too.)

31. Herbert Hoover

Okay.

Now, under the bell's cool edge is a giant owl who's a little chilly, too. So he's dressed in a fur coat, and he wants to attract your attention to it. He's saying, **"Whooooo...fur."**

"Whooooo...fur" for Hoover.

73

Franklin D. Roosevelt

1882-1945   President 1933-1945

Roosevelt is the only President to have served more than two terms. He was elected four times, and died early in his fourth term. His "New Deal" programs drew many attacks and enemies, but was overwhelmingly popular among the voters, who felt he was trying to help them during the Great Depression of the 1930s. FDR led the country through all but the last few months of World War II.

Franklin Roosevelt was a distant cousin of Teddy Roosevelt's, who gave away the bride when Franklin married his cousin, Eleanor. He contracted polio in 1921, and spent the rest of his life navigating in a wheel chair or on crutches. Roosevelt appointed the first woman cabinet member—Frances Perkins as Secretary of Labor. In 1939, he became the first President to appear on TV.

32. Franklin D. Roosevelt

The giant owl decides to take a stroll to warm up. He walks down a road made out of a twenty-foot wide brown belt that stretches into the horizon. As you can easily see, it's a **road belt**.

Road belt
for Roosevelt.

Harry S Truman

1884-1972

President 1945-1953

After taking office upon the death of FDR, Truman gave the final go-ahead for the U.S. to drop the atomic bombs on Japan. When the war was over, he pushed for the massive foreign aid that helped rebuild our friends and our former enemies alike. This American effort—one of the most generous in the history of the world—was called the Marshall Plan, after Truman's Secretary of State George Marshall. The scrappy Truman kept two plaques inscribed with mottos on his desk: "The buck stops here," and "If you can't stand the heat, get out of the kitchen."

When Truman chose to run for his own term in 1948, he was a heavy underdog to Republican Thomas Dewey. He won in a big upset with an aggressive campaign that won him the nickname "Give 'em hell Harry." Notice that the "S" in Harry S Truman doesn't have a period after it. That's because the letter wasn't an abbreviation for his middle name—it *was* his middle name.

33. Harry S Truman

At the end of the road belt, growing out of the large buckle, is a big tree with a face and arms—a **Tree Man**.

Tree Man
for Truman.

Dwight D. Eisenhower

1890-1969 President 1953-1961

Eisenhower was the allied commander in Europe during World War II, and was a popular hero. He was an extremely popular President, too, and even most Democrats had to agree with his campaign slogan, "I Like Ike." As President, he agreed to the Armistice that ended the Korean War, and he sent Federal troops to Arkansas to enforce integration at Little Rock's Central High School at the beginning of the modern Civil Rights movement.

In 1919, Eisenhower accompanied a convoy of army vehicles—including everything from a motorcycle to a tank—that crossed the U.S. from Washington D.C. to San Francisco. Roads were poor then—often just unpaved tracks—and the vehicles broke down often. It took the convoy from July 8 until September 5 to make the trip. No wonder that when he became President, Ike pushed for the establishment of the modern Interstate highway system!

Hang on!
The Tree Man is crawling up the side of a huge tower that has eyes on it. It must be the **Eyes-on Tower**!

Eyes-on Tower
for Eisenhower.

John F. Kennedy

1917-1963   President 1961-1963

Kennedy defeated Vice President Richard Nixon by the smallest margin ever. During his short administration, he had to deal with crises in Cuba, Germany, Southeast Asia and in our own Southern States, where the Civil Rights movement was running into violent opposition. Despite all these horrible problems, many Americans were smitten by the personal grace and glamour of the young President, his beautiful wife, Jacqueline, and their small children. Kennedy's assassination in Dallas remains the most vivid memory of millions of Americans.

Although Teddy Roosevelt was the youngest man ever to *be* President (remember why?), Kennedy was the youngest man ever *elected* President, at the age of 43. He was also the first President born in the twentieth century. He became the first President to appoint his brother to a cabinet post. Robert Kennedy was Attorney General. He remains the only President to win the Pulitzer Prize, for his book *Profiles in Courage.*

35. John F. Kennedy

On the very top of the tower is a bowl of **candy** (no wonder the Tree Man was climbing it).

Candy
for Kennedy.

There are **thirty-five** pieces of candy in the bowl. So you can easily remember that Kennedy was the **thirty-fifth** President!

Lyndon Johnson

1908-1973

President 1963-1969

Johnson had been one of John Kennedy's opponents for the Democratic nomination in 1960. Defeated at the convention, he agreed to run for Vice President, and he became President when Kennedy was killed. He fought for the passage of the Civil Rights Act of 1964, and he is known as the architect of "The Great Society," a series of social programs to reduce poverty and improve living conditions among the poor. He also made the decision to involve the United States deeply in the Vietnam War. Because of the divisions caused by strong opposition to the war, he decided not to run for another term in 1968.

Johnson was three months old before his parents gave him a name. As an adult, he was known as "LBJ," and the initials were shared by everyone in his family. Mrs. Johnson's real name was Claudia, but she was always known as Lady Bird. The Johnsons' two daughters were named Luci Baines and Lynda Bird. Even the dog got into the act. His name was Little Beagle Johnson. Needless to say, when they were home in Texas, they lived on the LBJ ranch.

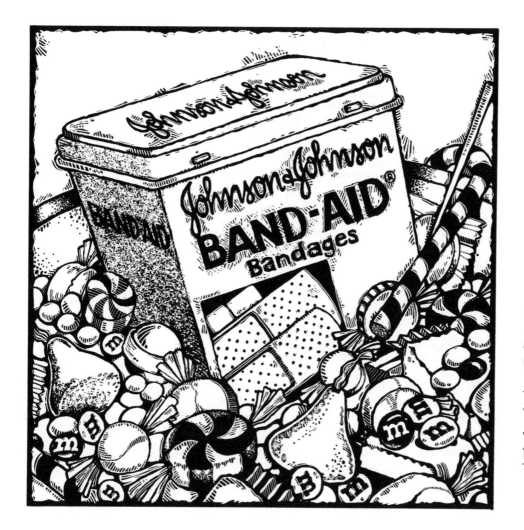

Inside the bowl of candy, mixed in with the goodies, is a **Johnson & Johnson**™ bandages box.

Johnson & Johnson
for Johnson.

Richard Nixon

1913-1994

President 1969-1974

Nixon barely lost the 1960 election to John Kennedy, but he came back to defeat Hubert Humphrey in 1968. His trip to China in 1972 shocked many of his strongly anti-Communist supporters. The United States landed the first man on the moon during Nixon's administration. Nixon is the only President to have resigned the office. He quit to avoid impeachment over his role in the Watergate scandal.

In college Nixon was a champion debater and an enthusiastic but not very good football player. He didn't play much, but toward the end of games, his classmates would start to chant, "Nixon! Nixon!" and when the coach sent him in for a few minutes, everyone would cheer. He was a very good poker player, and returned from his stint in the Navy during World War II with several thousand dollars in winnings.

If you look closely, you'll see that the bandage box has little **nicks on** it.

Nicks on
for Nixon.

Gerald Ford

1913-   President 1974-1977

Gerald Ford became President when Nixon resigned. He had been appointed Vice President when Spiro Agnew, the elected Vice President, was forced to resign when he was accused of taking bribes, so he was the only totally unelected President of the United States. One of Ford's first acts was to pardon Nixon for any criminal acts he may have committed as President. Although Ford was a likable and honest man, this hurt him when he sought election in 1976, and he was defeated.

While he was President, Ford earned a reputation as a physically awkward and clumsy man because of a few public missteps. Actually, he was one of the finest athletes ever to hold the office. He'd been an excellent football player at the University of Michigan, and was offered contracts by the Detroit Lions and the Green Bay Packers. During law school at Yale, he became Yale University's head boxing coach and an assistant football coach.

38. Gerald Ford

With a magnifying glass you examine one of the nicks. To your amazement, you see driving out of it a tiny **Ford**™ car.

Ford
for Ford.

Jimmy Carter

1924-

President 1977-1981

Carter won a very close election against Gerald Ford. He worked hard, pushed for human rights around the world, took very strong environmental stands, and got Egypt and Israel to agree to the Camp David Accords, which resulted in peace between the two old enemies. But Carter is remembered by many Americans as a failure because of an economic downturn during his term, and because of his inability to free the hostages taken from our embassy in Iran.

Although he uses his nickname Jimmy officially, Carter's full name is James Earl Carter, Jr. He was the first President born in a hospital (hard to believe, isn't it?). An avid woodworker, Carter often travels to various cities where he helps to build or remodel housing for those who have none through the program, Habitat for Humanity. He established the Carter Center to work for health, peace and freedom around the world, and has been called our most successful former President. In 2002, he won the Nobel Peace Prize.

Watch out!
The Ford car runs into a grocery **cart**, throwing groceries everywhere.
(Luckily, no one is hurt.)

Cart
for Carter.

Ronald Reagan

1911-

President 1981-1989

Largely because of the skills he learned as an actor, Reagan was known as "the Great Communicator" for his ability to get his points across to voters. During his administration spending on social programs was cut dramatically, and defense spending was greatly increased. Although his administration was marred by the Iran-Contra scandal, Reagan remained one of the most popular Presidents in American history. He appointed the first woman justice—Sandra Day O'Connor—to the Supreme Court.

Ronald Reagan was known as "Dutch" when he began as a radio sportscaster. He turned to a political career in the 1960s after making 54 movies in Hollywood, and he was elected Governor of California in 1966. Reagan often recalled that when he was a teenaged lifeguard, he saved 77 people from drowning. When he was inaugurated, he was only a few months younger than Dwight Eisenhower was when he left office—and Eisenhower had been the oldest President up to that point. Reagan is the only President to have been divorced. His first wife was the actress Jane Wyman.

As the groceries fly through the air, they turn into **ray guns** shooting out laser beams.

Ray guns
for Reagan.

It takes a lot of energy to turn groceries into ray guns. In fact, it takes **forty** gigawatts of electricity. Which is a coincidence, because Reagan was the **fortieth** President.

MILK

George Bush

1924-   President 1989-1993

George Bush was the first President since Martin Van Buren to be elected President right after serving as Vice President. During his term, the Soviet Union collapsed, East and West Germany united, and the Cold War between the totalitarian East and the democratic West ended in a definite Western victory. Bush was immensely popular after he engineered Desert Storm—the international effort to kick Iraqi dictator Saddam Hussein out of Kuwait. Bush had something else in common with Van Buren, though. His popularity plummeted when the economy went bad, and he was defeated in his attempt for reelection.

Bush enlisted in the Navy shortly after Pearl Harbor, and when he completed his training at the age of 19, he was the youngest flier in the U.S. Navy. In 1944, his Avenger was shot down by Japanese fire, and Bush had to bail out. He was rescued at sea by an American submarine.

The beams from the ray guns blast into a **bush** catching it on fire.

Bush
for Bush.

Bill Clinton

1946-

President 1993 –2001

Bill Clinton, whose middle name is Jefferson, is the first President to have been born after the Second World War. He will be remembered as the second President to be impeached. Like Andrew Johnson before him, he was found not guilty by the Senate of "high crimes and misdemeanors." Clinton's trial was televised in its entirety, riveting the nation.

When Clinton was first elected, England's ancient Oxford University flew the Stars and Stripes. How come? Clinton had studied at Oxford as a Rhodes Scholar and had just become the first Oxford man ever to be elected President of the U.S.

Hillary Rodham Clinton was elected to the Senate from New York as her husband's second term neared its end. She is the first President's wife to be elected to national office.

42. Bill Clinton

The smoke from the burning bush forms a whole bunch of numbers as it rises. All of the smokey numbers are dark and sooty, except for the ten, which isn't dirty at all. In fact, it's actually bright and shiny...it's a **clean ten**.

Clean ten
for Clinton.

George W. Bush

1946 –   President 2001-

George W. Bush is the second President's son to be elected President. Can you remember the first? "W" is also the first President to have been a major league baseball team owner. He was the managing general partner of the Texas Rangers before being elected Governor of Texas in 1994. Bush has degrees from both Yale (Bachelor of Arts) and Harvard (Master of Business Administration). He didn't gain as many overall votes as his opponent, Al Gore, in the 2000 Presidential election, but after a bitter dispute in Florida, he emerged the victor in electoral votes. Like his father, Bush has become a "war" President in the aftermath of the terrible events surrounding the terrorist attacks of September 11, 2001.

George W. Bush and his wife, Laura, own a ranch in Texas, where they sometimes entertain the leaders of other countries. Like his father, George W. likes to be physically active. He runs regularly, works on the property, and enjoys fishing for largemouth bass.

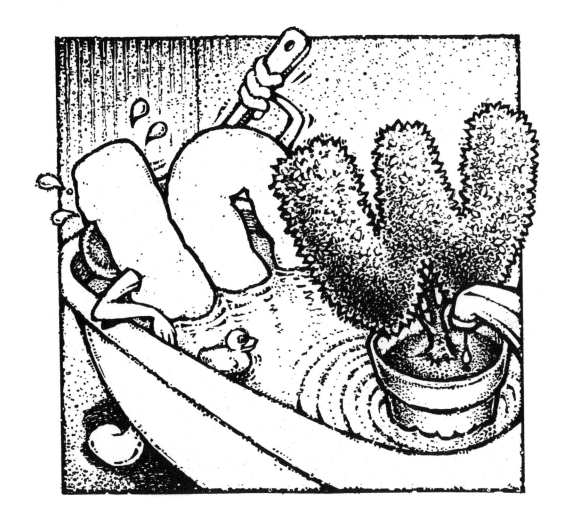

To stay bright and shiny, the clean ten likes to bathe in his tub, where the dripping faucet waters his potted plant . . . a **"W" bush**

"W" Bush

for George W. Bush.

Quiz #4

You've now done them all. Let's review them since Coolidge before you recite the whole list.

Who is standing under the cool edge and what does he say?

Where does the owl start walking?

Who is growing out of the buckle at the end of the road belt?

Where does the Tree Man start to climb?

What is on top of the tower of eyes?

How many pieces of candy are in the bowl?

   (What number President is Kennedy?)

What is in the bowl along with the candy?

What does the bandage box have all over it?

With a magnifying glass, what do you see coming out of the nicks?

What does the Ford crash into?

What do the groceries turn into?

How much energy does it take to turn the groceries into ray guns?

   (What number President is Reagan?)

What do ray guns shoot at?

What kind of bright and shiny number does the smoke from the burning bush make?

What kind of plant is growing in the bathtub?

SPLENDID!

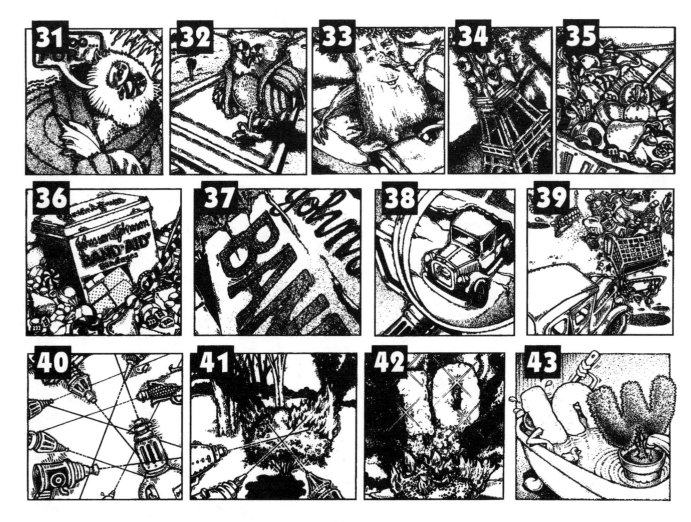

Quiz #5

Before you recite all the Presidents to yourself, let's do one more little review.

Who was the fifth President?
(Remember what the five dollar bill is doing.)

Who was the tenth?
(How old did we decide boys are
when they start wearing ties?)

Now, who was the twelfth?
(Start with the tenth, then use the pictures
in your mind to move two forward.)

Who was the thirty-fifth?
(Normally, you'd get this much candy
on Halloween.)

Who was the twentieth?
(How many cigars in the box?)

Go get 'em!

Who was the twenty-fifth?
(Billions and billions were sold.)

Who was seventeenth?
(Remember fifteen — what weighs fifteen pounds?
Then use the pictures in your mind to move two forward.)

Who was the thirty-third President?
(It has to be cold enough for certain things to happen, then
remember three more.)

Now, see if you don't know every one of the Presidents in
sequence, starting with the washing machine and coming all the
way up to the "W" bush growing in the bathtub. If you have
trouble, go back over the little quizzes a couple of times
and try again. Don't worry. You'll get it.

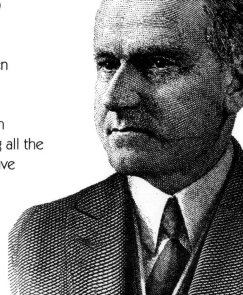

Yup.

Just For Fun

Here's a Jeopardy-style quiz to test what you've learned about the Presidents. We'll give you answers, and you come up with the questions. For example, if we say, "she sat on President Madison's clothes until he agreed to give her an interview," you have to say, "Who was that crazy newspaper lady who followed John Quincy Adams down to the Potomac?" Or something like that. ("Anne Royall" would also be acceptable, but we'd think you were showing off!)

Ready? Here we go. The answers—er, questions—are at the end. We'll start you off with a reeeely easy one.

1. After losing office, he ran for President again on the Know-Nothing ticket.

2. He was the first President who had never served in either the Continental Congress, the Senate or the House of Representatives.

3. He was President when the U.S. made the Louisiana Purchase.

4. Part of his jaw was replaced during a secret operation on a yacht in New York Harbor.

5. He was shot down in the Pacific during World War II.

6. This famous speech took only a minute or so to deliver.

7. As a boy, he watched the Battle of Bunker Hill.

8. He had made a fortune as a mining engineer before becoming President.

9. It was called "Mr. Madison's War."

10. He was the first President to have been born in a hospital.

11. He nominated George Washington to command American troops during the Revolution.

12. He was the first President born in the United States.

13. It was the war cry of those who wanted to fight Great Britain over the Oregon territory.

14. He was offered contracts to play professional football with both the Detroit Lions and the Green Bay Packers.

15. He was tone-deaf and he always said he only knew two tunes: "one is Yankee Doodle and the other isn't."

16. He was the primary author of the Declaration of Independence.

17. He was "Tippecanoe."

18. He was assassinated in Union Station by a man he'd refused to hire for a government job

19. He surrendered Fort Necessity.

20. He was the first President to throw out the first ball of the baseball season.

21. Their sons also became President.

22. He had 15 children—more than any other President.

23. He is the only President not renominated by his party when he wanted to run again.

24. The first telephone was installed in the White House during his administration.

25. The teddy bear was named after him.

26. He was the first President to have been born in a log cabin.

27. She dried the family laundry in the East Room of the White House.

28. He was the oldest man ever to serve in the office of President.

29. He was the only President who never married.

30. His grandfather had also been President.

31. He was President during "the Era of Good Feelings."

32. He was sworn into office by his father in the middle of the night.

33. They both died on July 4, 1826—the fiftieth anniversary of the proclamation of the Declaration of Independence.

34. He was the last Vice President before the elder George Bush to be elected President right after his Vice-Presidential term.

35. Before the Civil War, he was working in his brothers' leathergoods store for $50 a month.

36. He was the first President to have a radio in the White House.

37. He was the first President to have been born in the 20th century.

38. He was known as "the Father of the Constitution."

39. He was the only President who had also been Speaker of the House of Representatives.

40. In 1991, his body was exhumed and examined for the presence of poison.

41. He sent Lewis and Clark on their expedition.

42. He was called a baboon, a gorilla and an orangutan by his political opponents.

43. He is the only President to serve two non-consecutive terms.

44. He won fewer popular votes than his opponent and was only elected President after some Congressional hanky-panky.

45. He was known as "Old Hickory."

46. He is the only President to have been divorced.

47. He was the first President born in the 19th century.

48. He was the longest-lived of our Presidents—90 years, 9 months.

49. He was a corrupt New York politician who surprised everybody when he ran an honest Presidential administration.

50. He was wounded at the Battle of Trenton.

51. He is the only President to have won the Pulitzer Prize.

52. He was the only President who was ever impeached and tried by the Senate.

53. It was known as "Mr. Polk's war."

54. He was wounded in a duel, but killed his opponent.

55. It declared that the U.S. would not allow any European country to further colonize North or South America.

56. Its purchase was known as "Seward's Folly."

57. His nickname was "Ike."

58. His wife was known as "Lemonade Lucy" because she wouldn't allow wine or liquor in the White House.

59. He was the last President who had served in the Civil War.

60. He was known as "the President without a party."

61. She saved a portrait of George Washington when the British burned the White House.

62. Franklin Pierce's Vice-President, William R. King, was sworn in here.

63. He was the first President to die in office.

64. Our man Millard Fillmore lost the support of the Whig Party because he favored passage of this Act.

65. He was the heaviest of all our Presidents, at over 300 pounds.

66. He was the shortest and lightest President—5'4", 100 pounds.

67. He was our tallest President, at 6'4".

68. Thomas Jefferson's famous home.

69. He was known as "Old Rough and Ready."

70. Noted for his honesty, he said "a public office is a public trust."

71. Their fathers were also Presidents.

72. He was the first sitting member of the House of Representatives to be elected President.

73. He is the only former President to be elected to the Senate.

74. He brought Egypt and Israel together to sign the Camp David Accords.

75. He was angrily recalled as ambassador to France by George Washington.

76. He is the only President to have served more than two terms.

77. He is the only President to have resigned from office.

78. He was known as "Handsome Frank."

79. He was the Allied Commander in Europe during World War II.

80. Six states (North Dakota, South Dakota, Montana, Washington, Idaho and Wyoming) were admitted to the union during his term—more than during any other administration.

81. After losing office, he ran for President again on the Free Soil ticket.

82. She served the first Thanksgiving dinner at the White House.

83. He lived for 31 years after leaving office—longer than any other President.

84. He was the youngest man ever elected President.

85. He installed the first billiard table in the White House.

86. He was the last Revolutionary War veteran to become President.

87. He made a famous visit to Japan during Millard Fillmore's administration.

88. Years after serving as President, he was elected to the Congress of the Confederate States of America.

89. He was a sportscaster and an actor before he turned to politics.

90. Which President attended university in England?

91. He was the first true Presidential baseball fan.

92. He was the last President to have been born in a log cabin.

93. He polled more votes than Rutherford B. Hayes, but never became President.

94. He was the only President to have been born on the fourth of July.

95. He served in the House of Representatives after being President.

96. He was known as "Old Kinderhook."

97. He served the shortest term of any President.

98. He is known for his "Fourteen Points."

99. The Baby Ruth candy bar was named after her.

100. After leaving office, he was appointed Chief Justice of the Supreme Court.

101. Which President operated a major league baseball team?

102. He was the Union's most famous general.

103. He became President after John Kennedy's assassination.

104. He was nearsighted in one eye and farsighted in the other.

105. He was known as "Silent Cal."

106. He eloped with Zachary Taylor's daughter, Sarah.

107. He lost the use of his legs to polio and used a wheel chair or crutches.

108. He was the only President not to have been elected either President or Vice-President.

109. According to myth, he was President when the White House got its first bathtub with running water.

110. He was wounded during the Civil War and had four horses shot out from under him.

111. He was the first President married in the White House.

112. He was President during the Spanish-American War.

113. He was elected to his second term on the slogan, "He kept us out of war."

114. He was the first President to live in the White House.

? ? ? ? ?

1. Who was Millard Fillmore? (See? We told you the first one would be easy!)

2. Who was Zachary Taylor?

3. Who was Thomas Jefferson?

4. Who was Grover Cleveland?

5. Who is George Bush (the elder)?

6. What is Lincoln's Gettysburg Address?

7. Who was John Quincy Adams?

8. Who was Herbert Hoover?

9. What was the War of 1812?

10. Who is Jimmy Carter?

11. Who was John Adams?

12. Who was Martin Van Buren?

13. What was "Fifty-four forty or fight!"?

14. Who is Gerald Ford?

15. Who **was** Ulysses S. Grant?

16. Who was Thomas Jefferson?

17. Who was William Henry Harrison?

18. Who was James A. Garfield?

19. Who was George Washington?

20. Who was William Howard Taft?

21. Who are John Adams and George Bush (the elder)?

22. Who was John Tyler?

23. Who was Franklin Pierce?

24. Who was Rutherford B. Hayes?

25. Who was Theodore Roosevelt?

26. Who was Andrew Jackson?

27. Who was Abigail Adams?

28. Who is Ronald Reagan?

29. Who was James Buchanan?

30. Who was Benjamin Harrison?

31. Who was James Monroe?

32. Who was Calvin Coolidge?

33. Who were Thomas Jefferson and John Adams?

34. Who was Martin Van Buren?

35. Who was Ulysses S. Grant?

36. Who was Warren G. Harding?

37. Who was John F. Kennedy?

38. Who was James Madison?

39. Who was James K. Polk?

40. Who was Zachary Taylor?

41. Who was Thomas Jefferson?

42. Who was Abraham Lincoln?

? ? ? ? ?

43. Who was Grover Cleveland?

44. Who was Rutherford B. Hayes?

45. Who was Andrew Jackson?

46. Who is Ronald Reagan?

47. Who was Millard Fillmore?

48. Who was John Adams?

49. Who was Chester A. Arthur?

50. Who was James Monroe?

51. Who was John F. Kennedy?

52. Who was Andrew Johnson?

53. What was the Mexican War?

54. Who was Andrew Jackson?

55. What was the Monroe Doctrine?

56. What is Alaska?

57. Who was Dwight D. Eisenhower?

58. Who was Rutherford B. Hayes?

59. Who was William McKinley?

60. Who was John Tyler?

61. Who was Dolley Madison?

62. What is Cuba?

63. Who was William Henry Harrison?

64. What was the Fugitive Slave Act?

65. Who was William Howard Taft?

66. Who was James Madison?

67. Who was Abraham Lincoln?

68. What is Monticello?

69. Who was Zachary Taylor?

70. Who was Grover Cleveland?

71. Who are John Quincy Adams and George W. Bush?

72. Who was James A. Garfield?

73. Who was Andrew Johnson?

74. Who is Jimmy Carter?

75. Who was James Monroe?

76. Who was Franklin Roosevelt?

77. Who was Richard Nixon?

78. Who was Franklin Pierce?

79. Who was Dwight D. Eisenhower?

80. Who was Benjamin Harrison?

81. Who was Martin Van Buren?

82. Who was Sarah Polk?

83. Who was Herbert Hoover?

84. Who was John F. Kennedy?

85. Who was John Quincy Adams?

86. Who was Andrew Jackson?

87. Who was Commodore Matthew Perry?

88. Who was John Tyler?

89. Who is Ronald Reagan?

90. Who is Bill Clinton?

91. Who was Andrew Johnson?

92. Who was James A. Garfield?

93. Who was Samuel J. Tilden of New York?

94. Who was Calvin Coolidge?

95. Who was John Quincy Adams?

96. Who was Martin Van Buren?

97. Who was William Henry Harrison?

98. Who was Woodrow Wilson?

99. Who was Ruth Cleveland, daughter of Grover?

100. Who was William Howard Taft?

101. Who is George W. Bush?

102. Who was Ulysses S. Grant?

103. Who was Lyndon Johnson?

104. Who was James Buchanan?

105. Who was Calvin Coolidge?

106. Who was Jefferson Davis, future President of the Confederacy?

107. Who was Franklin Roosevelt?

108. Who is Gerald Ford?

109. Who was Millard Fillmore?

110. Who was Rutherford B. Hayes?

111. Who was Grover Cleveland?

112. Who was William McKinley?

113. Who was Woodrow Wilson?

114. Who was John Adams?

Some More Memory Tricks

Now that you have read this book, you know the Presidents backwards and forwards and you know the number of each President. Sometimes it also helps to know when a particular President was serving in office. The following are just a couple of tricks that can help you.

You can figure out the last two digits of a year when all of the Presidents from Tyler (10) to McKinley (25) served by multiplying the President's number by four and adding one. For instance, Tyler started his term in 1841.

4 times 10 plus 1 equals 41.

McKinley's term ended in 1901, when he died.

4 times 25 plus 1 equals 101.

In fact, this trick will tell you when the following Presidents' terms began: Tyler (10), Polk (11), Taylor (12), Hayes (19), and Garfield (20). It tells you when the following Presidents' terms ended: Fillmore (13), Pierce (14), Buchanan (15), Lincoln (16), Johnson (17), Arthur (21), Cleveland (22), Harrison (23), Cleveland (24), and McKinley (25). Grant is the only one of the lot for whom the trick gives you a number in the middle of his term.

Another trick is that Franklin Roosevelt, the 32nd President, was elected in 1932.

How About You?

If you want to be President, you have to be at least 35 years old. And you can forget the job if you weren't born in the United States. Once you get elected, you won't actually be able to make laws. That's Congress's job. But you will be able to propose laws or veto ones that Congress passes that you don't like.

You'll be elected in November, like most previous Presidents, and you'll be sworn in, or inaugurated, on January 20. (Until the passage of the 20th amendment in 1933, Presidents didn't take office until the following March.) Here's the oath you will take: "I do solemnly swear (or affirm) that I will faithfully execute the Office of President of the United States, and will to the best of my ability, preserve, protect and defend the Constitution of the United States."

No matter how good a President you are, you can serve only two elected terms. This is the result of a Constitutional amendment proposed by people who were unhappy that Franklin Roosevelt was elected to four terms.

Once you're President, you'll be Commander in Chief of all U.S. Armed Services. This means that you can ride in a tank or a helicopter anytime you want. More important, it means that our armed forces will continue to be under civilian control.

What if you are impeached and convicted of "high crimes and misdemeanors" and tossed out of office? Your Vice President takes over, of course. What if he immediately resigns to accept a multi-million-dollar contract to play shortstop for the Boston Red Sox (I would, wouldn't you?)? Here's the Presidential succession after the Vice President: the Speaker of the House of Representatives, the president *pro tempore* of the Senate, the Secretary of State, the Secretary of the Treasury, the Secretary of Defense, the Attorney General, the Secretary of the Interior, the Secretary of Agriculture, the Secretary of Commerce, the Secretary of Labor, the Secretary of Health and Human Services, the Secretary of Housing and Urban Development, the Secretary of Transportation, the Secretary of Energy, and the Secretary of Education.

Bibliography

Blassingame, Wyatt. *The Look-It-Up Book of Presidents.* New York: Random House, 1990.

Bumann, Joan and Patterson, John. *All New Edition of Our American Presidents.* St. Petersburg, FL: Willowisp Press, 1993.

Cooke, Donald. *Atlas of the Presidents.* Maplewood, N.J. Hammond, 1977.

Feerick, John. *The First Book of Vice-Presidents of the United States.* Danbury, CT: Watts, 1977.

Fisher, Leonard. *The White House.* New York: Holiday Press, 1989.

Freidel, Frank. *The Presidents of the United States of America.* Washington, DC: White House Historical Association, 1989.

Gill, Nancy. *Electing our President.* Columbus, OH: Fearon Teaching Aids, 1991.

Kessler, Paula and Segal, Justin. *The Presidents Almanac.* Los Angeles: Lowell House, 1996.

Lindop, Edmund. *Presidents by Accident.* Danbury, CT: Watts, 1991.

O'Neill, Richard and Bryan, Antonia. *Presidents of the United States.* New York: Smithmark, 1996.

Pascoe, Elaine. *First Facts About the Presidents.* Woodbury, CT: Blackbirch Press, 1996.

Provenson, Alice. *The Buck Stops Here: The Presidents of the United States.* San Diego, CA: Harcourt Brace, 1997.

Smith, Carter, ed. *Sourcebooks on the U.S. Presidency series.* Brookfield, CT. Millbrook Press, 1993.

Sullivan, Steve. *Mr. President: A Book of U.S. Presidents.* New York: Scholastic Inc., 1998.

Weber, Michael, Steins, Richard and Lucas, Eileen. *The Complete History of Our Presidents.* Vero Beach, FL: Rourke Corporation, 1997.

Index